Y0-ADX-325

Charphelia Company
15507 S. Normandie Ave., # 478
Gardena, CA 90247- 4028

Tel (323) 757-9050
Fax (323) 755-9222
email: admin@charphelia.com

SAN 254-6248

charphelia
Member NSSEA

Here is your sample copy of our new **Kwanzaa for Young People (and Everyone else!)** K-6 teacher-parent resource book/CD package.

Building upon the success of our award winning **Kwanzaa for Young People** audio CD (sample also enclosed), we've created the program to further extend its usefulness in classroom and home-study environments. The program includes an expanded version of the CD (with additional accompaniment versions of the selections for sing-along), packaged inside a newly created 52 page companion teacher-parent resource book. In addition to the holiday season it may be promoted during African American History Month, and throughout the year as a tool for general character education.

SRP for the new product is $19.95. Dealer discount is 50%. The original stand-alone CD remains available with a $12.99 SRP and a $7.79 dealer cost. Orders of $59.00 or more receive free shipping (lower forty eight US states only).

We encourage you to order in time for teachers to use the materials in their pre-holiday classroom and school activities.

We trust that you will recognize the need this wonderful resource fulfills and choose to offer it. Please feel free to call or email me with any questions.

Sincerely,

Charles Mims
admin@charphelia.com
Toll Free Tel: 888-299-2650

KWANZAA
for Young People (and Everyone else!)

K-6 Resource Book with Award-Winning CD

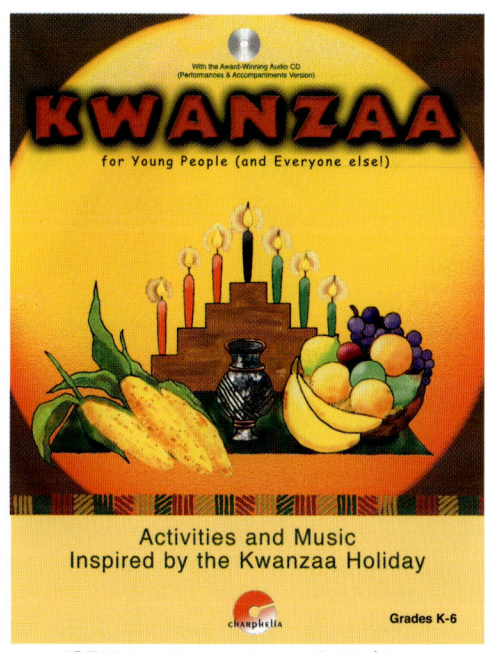

With the Award-Winning Audio CD
(Performances & Accompaniments Version)

- **Teachers' Choice** Award
- **Parent Council** Award
- **Parents' Choice** Award
- **Kid's First** Award
- **Los Angeles Unified School District Recommended Resource**

Available from
Charphelia Company
and
Baker & Taylor

ISBN 0-9713831-1-1   SRP $19.95

Engage students with coordinated activities and music in an exploration of the Kwanzaa holiday and its seven principles. Along the way they'll learn positive life-skills lessons which will aid them in the development of cultural awareness, self-esteem and ethical behavior.

preview songs online at
www.charphelia.com

Program includes **52 page resource book** written by National Board Certified, Disney Teacher-of-the-Year honoree Geanora Bonner, and *expanded version* of the award-winning **Kwanzaa for Young People (and Everyone else!) CD** with full performances and accompaniments.

CD Features
- musical selections for each day/principle of Kwanzaa
- full performances and accompaniments for easy sing-along
- simple, clear lyrics for easy understanding of concepts & pronunciations

Resource Book Features
- study sheets on the history & cultural practices of Kwanzaa
- creative, interdisciplinary activities for each day/principle of Kwanzaa
- lyrics, definitions & assessments

Charphelia Company, 15507 South Normandie Ave., # 478, Gardena, CA 90247
Toll Free Tel (888) 299-2650 • Fax (323) 755-9222 • www.charphelia.com

Charphelia Company
15507 S. Normandie Ave., # 478
Gardena, CA 90247-4028
Toll Free Tel (888) 299-2650
fax (323) 755-9222

charphelia
Member NSSEA

SAN: 254-6248

KWANZAA

for Young People (and Everyone else!)

www.charphelia.com

BILL TO: _____

SHIP TO: _____

_____

_____

_____

_____

_____

_____

_____

_____

PHONE: _____

PO #: _____

ORDER DATE: _____

ACCOUNT #: _____

ITEM #	PRODUCT TITLE	UNITS IN CASE	UNIT COST	CASE COST	UNIT QUANTITY	CASE QUANTITY	COST
70001	"Kwanzaa for Young People (Audio CD)	6	$7.79 (= 40% Discount)	$46.74			
85126	"Kwanzaa for Young People (Resource Book with CD)	6	$9.98 (= 50% Discount)	$59.88			

ITEM # 70001 SRP = $12.99

ITEM # 85126 SRP = $19.95

SUB TOTAL

SHIP

TOTAL

TERMS:
- NO MINIMUM ORDER REQUIRED
- PAYMENTS WITH CHECK (made payable to **Charphelia**), CASH, C.O.D., OR ACCEPTED CREDIT CARDS
- ESTABLISHED ACCOUNTS (WITH CREDIT APPROVAL) NET 30
- *CREDIT REFERENCES MUST BE ATTACHED TO ORDER FOR NET 30 CONSIDERATION
- FREIGHT ALLOWANCE: **FREE SHIPPING** ON ORDERS OF $59 OR MORE (lower 48 US states only)
- SHIPPING BILLED AT COST

PRICES EFFECTIVE AUGUST 1, 2002. ALL PRICES SUBJECT TO CHANGE WITHOUT NOTICE.

KWANZAA
for Young People (and Everyone else!)

**Activities and Music
Inspired by the Kwanzaa Holiday**

Grades K-6

Written by Geanora Bonner
Additional Activities by Vaughn Fuller, Charles Mims and Greg Martin
Music and Lyrics by Charles Mims and Patsy Moore
(except "Nia" by Vaughn Fuller and Charles Mims)

Charphelia Publications

> **Acknowledgments**
> The editors wish to extend a special thank-you to Jeri Boyles, Lenardo Dedman, Sandy Schuckett of the California School Librarians Association, Cassandra Will of St. Augustine Religious Education, Racquel Williams, and to Carolvee Beckstrand, Michelle Bell, Barbara Jones, Margaret Starks, Catherine Sumpter and Denise Webb of the Bret Harte Preparatory School in Los Angeles. These individuals generously provided creative input, editorial suggestions and feedback derived from classroom testing which contributed greatly to the quality of this program.
>   We also wish to acknowledge Dr. Maulana Karenga for having created Kwanzaa, and for his continuing contributions to our cultural enrichment.

Editor: Charphelia Editorial Committee
Cover and Book Design: Amy Shiotani
Cover Illustration: Yayoi Otani
Additional Graphics: Geanora Bonner

CD Credits

Producer: Charles Mims
Associate Producer: Patsy Moore
Executive Producers: Charles Mims and Greg Martin

Vocal Arrangements: Charles Mims and Patsy Moore

Adult Singers: Kenya C. Hathaway and Michael Mishaw
Adult Chanter on "Nia": Vaughn Fuller
Children Singers: Iman Burks, Lamont Cobb, Cecilia Gandy, Kierstin Gandy, Brandon Lucas, Shalah Williams
Children Singers' Conductor / Coordinator: Patrick Gandy
"Ujamaa" Actors: (Karen) Kierstin Gandy, (Father) Patrick Gandy, (Michael) Brandon Lucas, (Mother) Patsy Moore
Standout Child on "Kujichagulia": Cecilia Gandy
Piccolo, Alto Flute, Saxes: Jeff Clayton
Oboe, English Horn: Greg Martin
Keyboards, Programming: Charles Mims
Additional Percussion Programming: Vaughn Fuller

Engineer: John Ugarté at The Track House / Van Nuys, CA
Mastering: Louis F. Hemsey at GKS / Hollywood, CA
Art & CD Design: Amy Shiotani
Illustrations: Yayoi Otani

ISBN 0-9713831-1-1
Copyright © 2002 by Charphelia
All rights reserved.   Printed in USA

Copies of student pages may be reproduced by the individual teacher for home or classroom use only, not for commercial resale. No part of this publication may be reproduced for storage in a retrieval system, or transmitted in any form or by any means – electronic, mechanical, recorded, etc.– without the prior written permission of the publisher. Reproduction of these materials for an entire school or school system is strictly prohibited.

No part of the CD may be reproduced by any means, for any purpose. Unauthorized duplication is a violation of applicable laws.

Send all inquiries to:
Charphelia
15507 S. Normandie Ave., # 478
Gardena, CA 90247 - 4028

TABLE OF CONTENTS

The Beginnings of Kwanzaa	1
The Kwanzaa Holiday / The Seven Principles	2
The Kwanzaa Symbols	3
First Principle **Umoja**	4
Second Principle **Kujichagulia**	10
Third Principle **Ujima**	16
Fourth Principle **Ujamaa**	22
Fifth Principle **Nia**	28
Sixth Principle **Kuumba**	32
Seventh Principle **Imani**	38
"Kwanzaa Dance" Lyrics	44
Kwanzaa for Young People Quizzes	46
Kwanzaa Journal (for student reflections)	48

CD SELECTIONS

Full Performances:
1. **Umoja** - A children's chorus introduces us to the first principle of Umoja which means *unity*. We learn the importance of pulling together as a peaceful, global community.
2. **Kujichagulia** - Kujichagulia means *self-determination*. This song affirms the notion of uniqueness within each of us by maintaining that everyone has the power to decide his or her own destiny.
3. **Ujima** - The third principle of Ujima prepares young community members for *collective work and responsibility* because, as a West African proverb says, "Rain does not fall on one roof alone."
4. **Ujamaa** - Ujamaa is *cooperative economics*. Two stories help young listeners see the importance of supporting and giving back to our communities.
5. **Nia** - Nia means *purpose*. The African tradition of "call and response" is used in this chant which explains that we all have a purpose and need to plan for our success.
6. **Kuumba** - This song encourages us not only to celebrate, express and accept all forms of Kuumba *(creativity)* around us, but also to share our creations with the world.
7. **Imani** - Imani means *faith*. Faith happens on many levels. This song encourages faith that flows in, through, around and beyond; a faith in ourselves, in family and in God; a faith that will endure.
8. **Kwanzaa Dance** - No celebration is complete without some dancing music. This lively song concludes with a chant of the seven principles.

Accompaniments:
9. **Umoja**
10. **Kujichagulia**
11. **Ujima**
12. **Nia**
13. **Kuumba**
14. **Imani**
15. **Kwanzaa Dance**

note: *there is no accompaniment version of Ujamaa*

KWANZAA

The Beginnings of Kwanzaa

Dr. Maulana Karenga wanted to find a way for African Americans to return to a sense of pride in their culture and history. He had a dream of a special time when people could remember and celebrate.

While a college student during the 1960's, he began to study harvest ceremonies and festivals from all parts of the continent of Africa. For groups of people around the world, planting seeds, taking care of those plants and gathering the crops (harvesting) is a hard but necessary task for the whole community. Everyone has to work together to make sure there is food for the entire tribe. The men of the village may clear the land of trees and bushes. The women may have to carry buckets from far away to water the crops. Small children may have to go through the fields and remove harmful pests from plants. Older children may have to stand guard and make sure larger animals don't ruin the crops. Everyone has work to do so they can all eat. When the harvest is in, everyone is rewarded for their hard work. Usually the reward is a large festival or party for the whole community.

All of the tribes that Dr. Karenga studied celebrated their harvests in slightly different ways, but he was looking at the things they did that were alike. The harvests usually lasted several days. The people would take a break from their work and attend a ceremony. There were prayers offered by the chief or king of the tribe and special honors were given to the tribe's ancestors. Then there was a celebration with feasting, music and dancing. It was a time set aside for everyone to remember all that they had done to help the tribe have a good harvest. It was also a time for them to think about and plan what they would do in the next year to make the future harvest even better.

Dr. Karenga created Kwanzaa in 1966. It is celebrated each year from December 26 through January 1. "Kwanza" is the Swahili word for *first*. He added an "a" to the word to name the holiday. He thought of the holiday as being a celebration of first fruits. He wanted it to be a time of healing, a time of celebration, a time of thinking and a time of planning that would last throughout the year.

Questions

1. Who created Kwanzaa?
2. What continent's harvest ceremonies and festivals did Dr. Karenga study?
3. In what year was Kwanzaa created?
4. What does "harvesting" mean?
5. According to Dr. Karenga, what does the Kwanzaa holiday celebrate?

© Charphelia Publications

The Kwanzaa Holiday

Kwanzaa is a cultural holiday which lasts for seven days (December 26 through January 1) and includes seven principles (one for each day). The principles are given special attention during the holiday and they are also important throughout the year. Each principle has a Swahili name. Swahili is a language spoken throughout many parts of Africa. It is the language used for all of the special words of Kwanzaa.

Each night family and friends gather to light one of seven symbolic candles and to share thoughts about the principle of that day. On the sixth night of Kwanzaa a feast called the *Karamu* (ka-RAH-moo) is held. This is a joyous affair where people of the community gather to celebrate with food, music, story-telling, speech-giving, dancing, and the exchanging of gifts.

The Seven Principles
(a black, red or green candle is lit on each of the seven days.)

1. **Umoja** (oo-MOH-jah)--**BLACK CANDLE (Dec. 26)**
   It means *unity*.

2. **Kujichagulia** (koo-gee-CHA-goo-LEE-ah)--**FIRST RED CANDLE (Dec. 27)**
   It means *self-determination*.

3. **Ujima** (oo-GEE-mah)--**FIRST GREEN CANDLE (Dec. 28)**
   It means *collective work and responsibility*.

4. **Ujamaa** ((oo-jah-MAH)--**SECOND RED CANDLE (Dec. 29)**
   It means *collective economics*.

5. **Nia** (NEE-ah)--**SECOND GREEN CANDLE (Dec. 30)**
   It means *purpose*.

6. **Kuumba** (koo-OOM-bah)--**THIRD RED CANDLE (Dec. 31)**
   It means *creativity*.

7. **Imani** (ee-MON-ee)--**THIRD GREEN CANDLE (Jan. 1)**
   It means *faith*.

Pronouncing Swahili Vowels

a is like the *ah* sound in *father*

e is like the *a* sound in *say*

i is like the *ee* sound in *see*

o is like the *o* sound in *so*

u is like the *oo* sound in *too*

© Charphelia Publications

The Kwanzaa Symbols

Seven basic symbols are used in Kwanzaa celebrations. They remind people of good things they have achieved during the year and can accomplish in the future. They also remind people of their ancestors and of different ideas about African culture.

The Seven Basic Symbols

1. **mazao** (mah-ZAH-o): ***Fresh fruits and vegetables*** representing the crops of the harvest and the rewards of hard work.
2. **mkeka:** (m-KAY-kah): The ***mat*** on which the other items are placed.
3. **kinara** (kee-NAH-rah): The seven-armed ***candle holder*** which holds the seven candles.
4. **muhindi** (moo-HEEN-dee): Ears of ***corn*** representing the children in the family or house.
5. **mishumaa saba** (mee-shoo-MAH-ah SAH-bah): The black, red and green ***candles*** which are placed in the kinara. There are seven in all to represent the seven Kwanzaa principles.
6. **kikombe cha umoja** (kee-KOM-bay cha-oo-MO-jah): The ***unity cup*** from which a liquid (usually juice or water) called a libation is poured to honor the ancestors.
7. **zawadi** (zah-WAH-dee): ***Gifts*** given, especially to children.

Two Additional Symbols:

1. **bendera** (bayn-DAY-rah): The black, red and green flag introduced by civil rights leader Marcus Garvey as the symbol for people of African ancestry around the world.

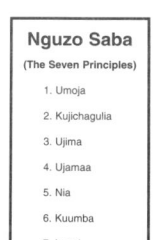

2. **Nguzo Saba Poster** (en-GOO-zo SAH-bah): A poster of the seven Kwanzaa principles. "Nguzo Saba" is Swahili for "seven principles."

Nguzo Saba
(The Seven Principles)
1. Umoja
2. Kujichagulia
3. Ujima
4. Ujamaa
5. Nia
6. Kuumba
7. Imani

© Charphelia Publications

Umoja
(CD TRACK 1)

Umoja means unity, you and me
Living together in
One big family
Umoja is unity, you and me
Living forever in
Love and harmony
Unity!

One wide blue sky above us
One bright yellow sun to light the days
One mother earth who holds us
Now doesn't it all just seem to say that

We are all one world
Why not be one heart and mind?
One community
That is what we're meant to be

One destiny before us
One candle tonight to light the way
One loud and happy chorus
That really has only this to say

We are all one world
Let's all be one heart and mind
One community
That is what we're meant to be

Umoja is unity, you and me
Living forever in
Love and harmony
Unity!

© Charphelia Publications

The first principle of Kwanzaa is *Umoja* (oo-MOH-jah)

Umoja = Unity

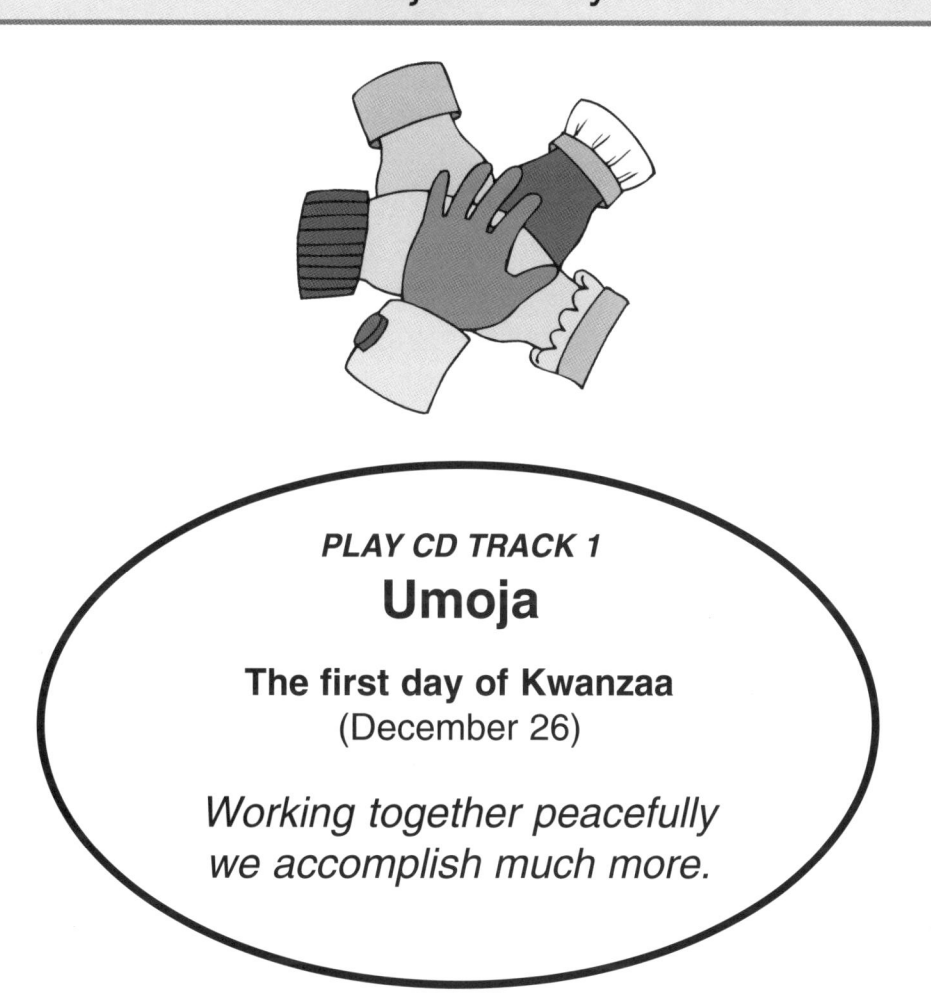

PLAY CD TRACK 1

Umoja

The first day of Kwanzaa
(December 26)

Working together peacefully we accomplish much more.

The song talks about "One wide blue sky..."

What other things do you share with each other and the rest of the world?

(Write your answer below)

© Charphelia Publications

Unity Chain Game

Teacher Directions

- Have students stand or sit side-by-side to form the *unity chain.*
- Whisper the *unity phrase* below to the first student in the chain. You may choose to use all or a portion of it.
- Instruct student to whisper the phrase to the next student, continuing the sequence until the last student has heard the phrase.
- Have the last student share the phrase aloud with the class. If it is correct discuss the role unity played in achieving success. If it is incorrect whisper the phrase to the last student and repeat the exercise in reverse order (from last student to first). This time have the first student share the phrase with the class. If still incorrect discuss how a more unified effort might have brought success.

Unity Phrase

Can you state, what was said
From my mouth, to your head
Say these words, perfectly
Demonstrate our unity!

© Charphelia Publications

Unity Collage
Teacher Directions

Materials for each student:
grid, crayons, scissors, sheet of construction paper, glue

Directions:
1. Have students draw on the reverse side of the grid to create an abstract work. They should fill the entire page.
2. Have them cut along grid lines to create nine equal pieces.
3. Collect the pieces, mix and redistribute nine pieces to each student.
4. Have students glue their new pieces to fashion a unique design on a piece of construction paper.
5. Have students combine their works to create a Unity Collage.

Grid

© Charphelia Publications

Song Puzzler

Fill in the missing words from the song *Umoja*.

1. Umoja means _____.

2. Living together in love and _____.

3. _____ bright yellow sun to light the _____.

4. We are _____ one _____.

5. Why not be one _____ and _____?

6. One _____ tonight to _____ the way.

7. That is what we're _____ to _____.

© Charphelia Publications

Teacher Directions

Extending into Music
- Reproduce lyric sheet for each student (page 4).
- Have students repeatedly sing "Umoja's" refrain ("Umoja means unity, you and me... Unity!"). One student should begin, then add voices until the entire group is singing.
- Encourage students to listen for the differences in sound produced by fewer and larger numbers of voices in *unison* (sounding the same musical note at the same time). Does the sound get louder or softer? In what other ways does the sound change (tone color, texture, etc.)?
- Consider recording students' singing for playback.

Vocabulary:
1. chorus
2. community
3. destiny
4. harmony
5. Umoja
6. unity

Explore Unity
- Have students discuss ways unity can benefit school life (classroom neatness, playground games, safety drills, etc.).

note: Vocabulary = words in the songs or activities that may need introduction, review or reinforcement.

Extending Unity...
...to the classroom: Plan a classroom unity activity such as "Wear a Purple Sock Day." Create a classroom slogan.
...to the family: Have students share what they enjoy doing with their families. Explore other opportunities to plan family activities.
...to the community: Have students research things that happen in the community and reflect unity. Can they think of other activities which might help build community unity?

© Charphelia Publications

Kujichagulia

(CD TRACK 2)

Kujichagulia
Self-determination
You have the power to decide now
Who you are

No one else could ever be you
You have something very special to do
Do that something for the world to see

You are someone with your very own name
You are someone with a purpose and aim
Be that someone and you'll find you are free

Who I'm gonna be
Is a choice for me
I decide my destiny

You are beautiful and made to be great
You have something wonderful to create
So express yourself outstandingly

Who I'm gonna be
Is a choice for me
I decide my destiny

Kujichagulia
Kujichagulia

© Charphelia Publications

The second principle of Kwanzaa is *Kujichagulia* (koo-gee-CHA-goo-Lee-ah)

Kujichagulia = Self-Determination

PLAY CD TRACK 2

Kujichagulia

The second day of Kwanzaa
(December 27)

*I can choose who I am,
what I will do and
what I will be.*

The song states "Who I'm gonna be is a choice for me..."

Name one or more choices you've made about your future.
(Write your answer below)

© Charphelia Publications

Kujichagulia Mask Directions

Masks are made and used all over the world. In Africa masks are used for special ceremonies and occasions. Make a special Kujichagulia mask. Use the suggestions below or make up your own shapes and messages!

1.
The **eyes** tell what you like to read:

Draw ⊕ ⊕ if you choose to read comics.

Draw ⊙ ⊙ if you choose to read magazines.

Draw ▭ ▭ if you choose to read books.

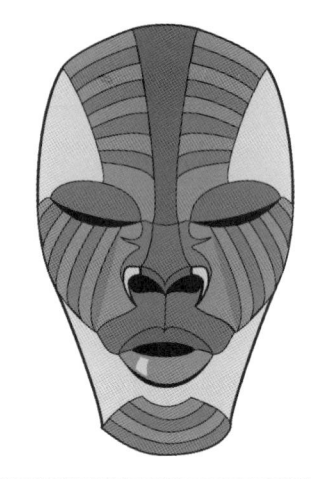

2.
The **nose** tells what you like to smell:

Draw 🔲 if you want to smell perfume.

Draw 🔘 if you want to smell baking cookies.

Draw 🔳 if you want to smell flowers.

3. Make up your own mouth for the mask. What does it tell about you?

4. Make up your own cheeks for the mask. What do they tell about you?

5. Make up your own chin for the mask. What does it tell about you?

6. Make up your own forehead for the mask. What does it tell about you?

Can you read your classmates' masks?

Can they read yours?

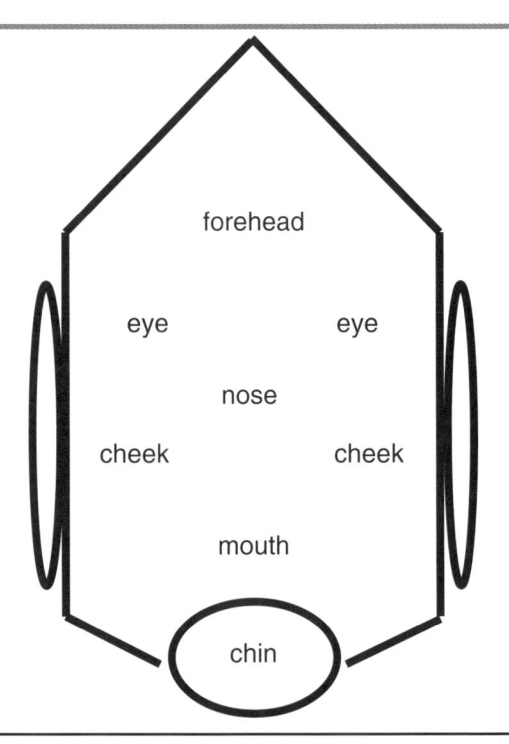

© Charphelia Publications

This smaller mask can help you place the parts on your large mask. Maybe you will turn your mask another way! Use bright colors to decorate your mask. Add hair if you want.

Kujichagulia Mask

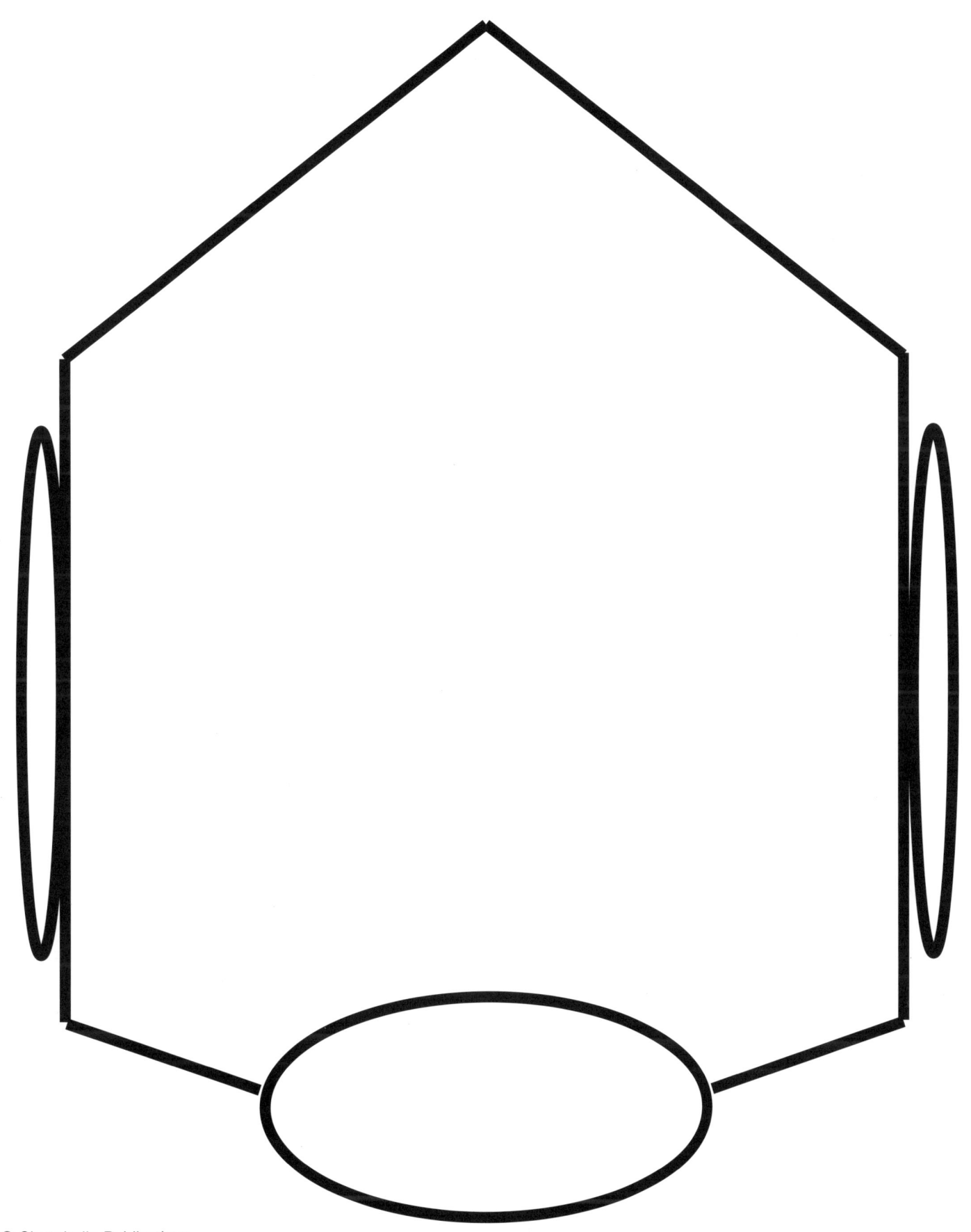

Share and Discuss

Self-Determination

Tell about your decision to achieve a goal.
For example, tell why and how you learned to ride a bike, play a musical instrument or earn a good grade. Or maybe you want to tell about a different goal that you achieved!

© Charphelia Publications

Teacher Directions

Extending into Music
Improvisation (the spontaneous creation of music during performance) allows performers to invent their own music and thereby exercise self-determination.
- **Play CD Track 2.**
- As the music plays, point to each student one at a time, encouraging them to improvise responses. They might sing melodies, clap rhythms, or rap lyrics.

Vocabulary:
1. aim
2. choice
3. decide
4. destiny
5. determination
6. Kujichagulia

Explore Self-Determination
- Have students make short and long-term goal statements.
- Instruct them to plan steps for completing one short-term goal.
- Encourage them to share.

Extending Self-Determination...
...to the classroom: Provide opportunities throughout the school day for students to make specific choices.
...to the family: Have individual students discuss their goal statements with their family. Have them identify family goals and plans that can then be shared with the class. How are families unique?
...to the community: Have students research ways in which goals are set in their community. How is planning done in the community? What makes their community unique? What choices in the community interest them?

© Charphelia Publications

Ujima

(CD TRACK 3)

Opening Refrain:

Ujima for our fathers and mothers - **HARMONY**
Ujima for our sisters and brothers - **HARMONY**
Ujima's whenever - **UNISON**
We help each other - **UNISON**
By working together - **UNISON**

Ujima is to understand - **HARMONY**
That everybody needs a hand - **UNISON**
Ujima's whenever - **UNISON**
We help each other - **UNISON**
By working together - **UNISON**

Never suppose it's true
What happens to you
Has no effect, whatsoever, on me
My friend, you see
That will never be

WHY?

We're all connected
We're intersected
That is the spirit of community
Cooperation
Now, that's the key

We help each other
By working together
We work together
By helping each other

For our fathers and mothers
For our sisters and brothers
Ujima's whenever
We help each other
By working together

Ujima is to understand
That everybody needs a hand
Ujima's whenever
We help each other
By working together

© Charphelia Publications

The third principle of Kwanzaa is *Ujima* (oo-GEE-mah))

Ujima = Collective Work and Responsibility

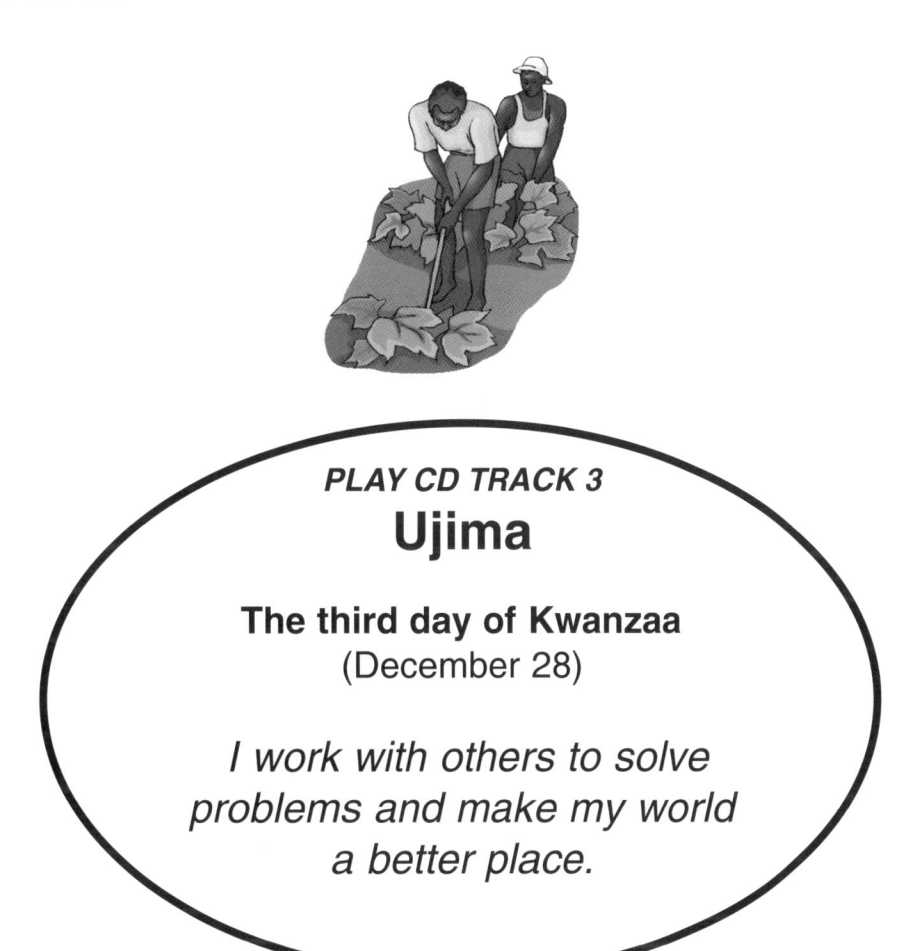

PLAY CD TRACK 3
Ujima

The third day of Kwanzaa
(December 28)

I work with others to solve problems and make my world a better place.

The song states "We help each other by working together..."

Name one or more ways you can help other people.
(Write your answer below)

© Charphelia Publications

Song Puzzler

Circle the correct words from the song *Ujima*.

1. Ujima is to *(understand, know)*.

2. That *(everybody, teacher)* needs a hand.

3. We help each other by *(playing, working)* together.

4. Never suppose it's *(true, blue)*.

5. What happens to *(them, you)*.

6. We *(scare, help)* each other.

© Charphelia Publications

UJIMA CRISS-CROSSWORD

Fill in each blank with the correct word from the puzzle to complete the sentence.

Example: "May I please have your <u>cooperation</u>," said the teacher.

1. Most girls want to be _____ when they grow up.

2. _____ is the third principle of Kwanzaa.

3. Peanut butter and jelly go well _____.

4. We have great school _____.

5. I have three _____ and one brother.

6. My two uncles are my mother's _____.

7. All _____ were once little boys.

8. In our _____ there are many houses.

```
                    c
                    o
          b  r  o  t  h  e  r  s        s
                    p                    i
                    e                    s
                    r                    t
          u  j  i  m  a                  e
                    t  o  g  e  t  h  e  r
                    i                    s
                    o
       c  o  m  m  u  n  i  t  y
                    ■
                    f
                    a
                    t
             m  o  t  h  e  r  s
                    e
                    r
                    s  p  i  r  i  t
```

© Charphelia Publications

Student Problem-Solving Cards

1. You have to carry your belongings across a river in a boat.

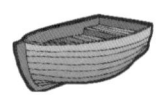

2. You have a lion, a zebra, and a bag of grass.

3. The lion eats zebras. The zebra eats grass. Luckily your lion is tame and will not eat you.

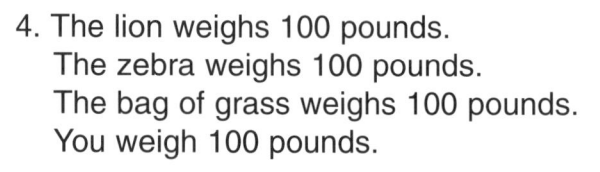

4. The lion weighs 100 pounds.
   The zebra weighs 100 pounds.
   The bag of grass weighs 100 pounds.
   You weigh 100 pounds.

5. Your boat can carry no more than two hundred pounds at a time (remember, you weigh 100 pounds).

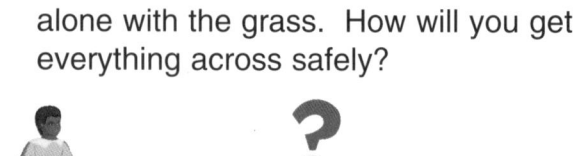

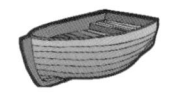

6. You cannot leave the lion alone with the zebra. You cannot leave the zebra alone with the grass. How will you get everything across safely?

Teacher Directions

- Reproduce and cut cards apart.
- Form groups of six students.
- Inform students that they are going to work together to solve a problem.
- Give each group member a different card.
- Help with hints if needed.

Read To Students Before Distributing Cards:

"You've completed an African safari where you collected animals for the local wildlife reserve. On the way back your truck breaks down. You need to reach camp by nightfall. A local villager guides you to a place from where you will be able to return. But there is a problem!"

Solution:
- Take the zebra across and leave it.
- Go back and get the grass.
- Bring the grass across and leave it. Take the zebra back with you.
- Leave the zebra. Take the lion across and leave it with the grass.
- Go back and get the zebra.
- Everything is across the river now.

© Charphelia Publications

Teacher Directions

Extending into Music
One of the ways instruments and voices "work together" in music is through the use of *harmony* (the playing or singing of two or more different musical notes at the same time).
- **Play CD Track 3.**
- Have students listen to the voices in the opening refrain section for contrasts between lines sung in harmony and unison (see lyric sheet, page 16).

Results: *Problem-Solving Cards*, page 20
- Share results
- Have students discuss the process they went through to complete the assignment.
- Ask students to consider what might have happened if they had not had all of the cards.
- Discuss the importance of working as a team.
- Have students review other ways in which they collaborate.

Vocabulary:
1. cooperation
2. intersected
3. responsibility
4. Ujima

Arts and Crafts Idea *(Found-Art Sculpture Day)*
- Have students sign up to collect and bring in items that can then be used to create sculptures (string, pebbles, leaves, scraps of cloth, etc.). Stress the importance of everyone making a contribution.

Extending Collective Work and Responsibility...
...to the classroom: Give students opportunities to take responsibility. Teach a lesson to a few and have them share the information with others.
...to the family: Have students discuss their household chores/duties. How do these responsibilities contribute to family order?
...to the community: Have students look for ways in which communities work together. Is there an opportunity for citizens to volunteer for public projects?

© Charphelia Publications

Ujamaa
(CD TRACK 3)

Story One

Karen:

I love orange juice! It's probably my favorite thing to drink in the whole wide world! Every morning, Daddy cuts big oranges into halves and squeezes them on this thing called a press. The juice is so delicious! Well, yesterday morning he told me that a woman named Madeline Turner invented the fruit press in 1916 so that people could easily squeeze more oranges than you usually can by hand. And guess what? She was from Oakland, California! That's where I live!

I told Daddy that I want to invent something one day that will help a lot of people the same way. And he said...

Father:

That's a fantastic idea Karen. You have quite an imagination and it's nice that you want to share it with others. We are all made stronger by helping others grow strong.

Karen:

And then we drank some of the best juice Daddy's ever squeezed! It makes me thirsty just thinking about it!

Story Two

Michael:

Do you know Mr. Jackson? He owns "Jackson's Market," two blocks up and one block over on Kessler Avenue. My family, like most of the other families in our neighborhood, has shopped there for years. In fact, we've bought sugar, and flour, and paper napkins, and bread and eggs, and [*deep breath*], lots of other things from Mr. Jackson for as long as I can remember!

My mother says...

Mother:

When Mr. Jackson does good business, it helps the entire community by providing jobs for some and goods for the rest of us.

Michael:

So... hmmm... I guess I should buy a candy bar everyday to help Mr. Jackson out?

Mother:

Uh... Michael? That's not exactly what I had in mind.

[*laughter*]

© Charphelia Publications

The fourth principle of Kwanzaa is *Ujamaa* (oo-jah-MAH))

Ujamaa = Cooperative Economics

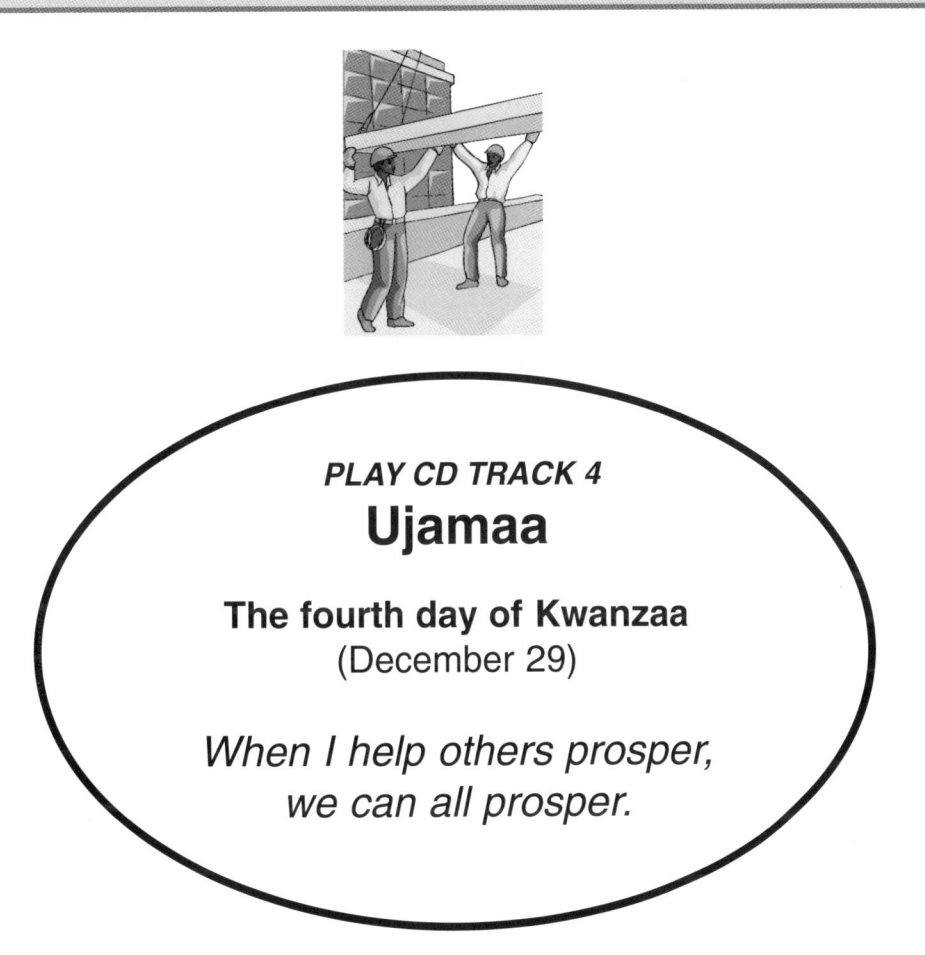

PLAY CD TRACK 4
Ujamaa

The fourth day of Kwanzaa
(December 29)

*When I help others prosper,
we can all prosper.*

Story Two says that, "When Mr. Jackson does good business, it helps the entire community by providing jobs for some and goods for the rest of us."

Name a business that helps your community and tell how it helps.

(Write your answer below)

© Charphelia Publications

Papier Mâché Banks

Materials:
- A two-liter plastic soda bottle for each student
- Newspaper
- Wallpaper paste or white glue diluted with equal parts water
- Tempera paints or colored markers
- Paint brushes
- Water
- Scissors or other cutting utensil (teacher only)

Directions:
- Write your name on the bottom of your bottle.
- To create strips, tear newspaper into pieces one to two inches wide.
- Submerge newspaper strips in paste or glue solution and remove excess solution from strips with fingers.
- Paste strips to soda bottle and smooth out with fingers until entire bottle is covered. Use at least three layers of strips.
- Allow bottles to dry.
- When bottles have dried, **teacher** should cut/punch coin slot in each bottle two to three inches from spout.
- Decorate bottles with paint or markers.

Suggestion: When your bank is full consider starting a savings account. Ask parents for suggestions. Consider saving for a future goal.

© Charphelia Publications

Ujamaa Word Hunt

Locate and circle the hidden words.

```
A C H A R I T Y O B D H Y E I
B R A X M E N W C U I Y D A K
Q P F K O T W Z I N V E S T W
V R J E G Z U I B M I A H U A
C O P C X F R C H A D C Q B N
S F G O I Z M O X P E Y C I Z
H I C L B R X M E V N L F N A
O T H L U J A M A A D R A Q A
C L S E H M Z U L A B O R O U
X W N C G E E N C R O U P G H
G O T T P A O I Y K F L U P S
O Q E I L V S T O B W D Q H T
O N R V U R I Y I S R W V P M
D U B E C O N O M I C S J L A
S T T X J Q K B U S I N E S S
```

HIDDEN WORDS:

BUSINESS	DIVIDEND	KWANZAA
CHARITY	ECONOMICS	LABOR
COLLECTIVE	GOODS	PROFIT
COMMUNITY	INVEST	UJAMAA

© Charphelia Publications

Teacher Page

Ujamaa Word Hunt
(solution)

```
A C H A R I T Y O B D H Y E I
B R A X M E N W C U I Y D A K
Q P F K O T W Z I N V E S T W
V R J E G Z U I B M I A H U A
C O P C X F R C H A D C Q B N
S F G O I Z M O X P E Y C I Z
H I C L B R X M E V N L F N A
O T H L U J A M A A D R A Q A
C L S E H M Z U L A B O R O U
X W N C G E E N C R O U P G H
G O T T P A O I Y K F L U P S
O Q E I L V S T O B W D Q H T
O N R V U R I Y I S R W V P M
D U B E C O N O M I C S J L A
S T T X J Q K B U S I N E S S
```

HIDDEN WORDS:

BUSINESS	DIVIDEND	KWANZAA
CHARITY	ECONOMICS	LABOR
COLLECTIVE	GOODS	PROFIT
COMMUNITY	INVEST	UJAMAA

© Charphelia Publications

Teacher Directions

Extending into Music
Musicians often practice cooperative economics by forming *ensembles* (bands, singing groups, etc.) that perform together to earn money.
- **Listen to CD Track 4.**
- Have students create their own accompaniment to a classroom performance of the two Ujamaa stories (page 22). They can use available or student-made percussion and pitched instruments (drums, tambourine, bells, etc.).
- You might pay your performers with some item they will perceive as reward (stickers, candy, fruit, etc.).

Demonstrate Cooperative Economics
Fund-Raising Activity
- Have students plan and carry out a fund-raising activity. Explain that they will be investing time and effort to earn a dividend. The profits should be used to fulfill a shared goal (donation to local charity, sponsor field trip, classroom "Karamu" feast, etc.).
- Suggestions for fund-raising: car wash, raffle, candy sale, bake sale, etc.

Note: "Karamu": The traditional feast held on December 31, the 6th day of Kwanzaa.

Vocabulary:
1. business
2. cooperation
3. economics
4. goods
5. prosper
6. Ujamaa

Results: *Fund-Raising Activity*
- Have students discuss what they learned from their fund-raising experience.
- Lead them in a discussion about the implications for business in general (division of labor, profit and loss, investment, supplier, distributor, customer, etc.).
- What ideas might they have for how business and their community work together to help each other?
- How might they help each other and their community through their own future business efforts?

Extending Cooperative Economics...
...to the classroom: Help children to see relationship between investing time in their work and the dividends of increased knowledge and strong grades.
...to the family: Have students discuss saving and spending with their families.
...to the community: Students can locate local merchants and business people to interview about the interdependent relationship between business and community.

© Charphelia Publications

Nia
(CD TRACK 5)

Leader:	Say *N*
Chorus:	*N*
Leader:	Say *I*
Chorus:	*I*
Leader:	Now say *A*
Chorus:	*A*
Leader:	What does it spell ?
Chorus:	Nia
Leader:	What does it spell ?
Chorus:	Nia
Leader:	And what does it mean ?
Chorus:	Purpose
Leader:	What does it mean ?
Chorus:	Purpose
Leader:	Nia means purpose Nia means purpose Nia means purpose Say Nia means purpose
Chorus:	Nia means purpose Nia means purpose Nia means purpose Nia means purpose
Leader:	Who has a purpose ?
Chorus:	We have a purpose
Leader:	Who has a purpose ?
Chorus:	You have a purpose
All:	We all have a purpose We all have a purpose (repeat)

© Charphelia Publications

The fifth principle of Kwanzaa is *Nia* (NEE-ah)

Nia = Purpose

PLAY CD TRACK 5
Nia

The fifth day of Kwanzaa
(December 30)

I have plans for my future success and I help others succeed too.

The chant says "We all have a purpose..."

What is your purpose as a student?
What is your purpose as a family member?
(Write your answers below)

© Charphelia Publications

Nia Drum Circle Maze

A drum circle is a small or large gathering of people that drum, dance, and sing together. Your purpose is to help the master drummer at the top of the maze find the path to join his fellow musicians. Draw a line showing him the way.

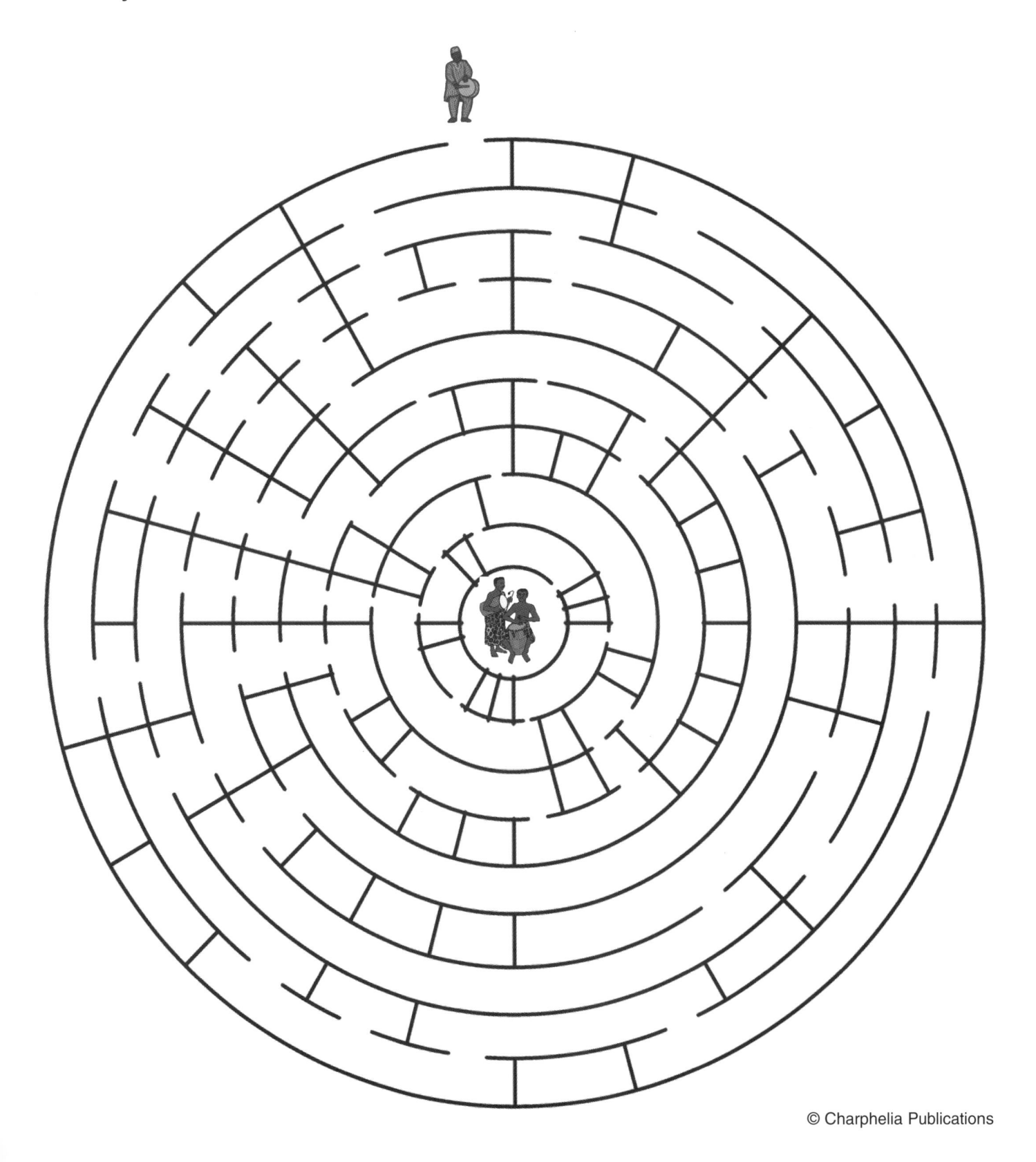

© Charphelia Publications

Teacher Directions

Extending into Music
- **Listen to CD Track 5.**
- Explain to students that this is a *call and response* (alternation between two performers or groups of performers, especially between a soloist and group. It is based on an ancient African musical form).
- Divide class into "Leader" and "Chorus" and perform "Nia" (page 28).
- Have students use percussion to self-accompany.
- Discuss with students what might be the purpose of the leader versus the chorus (i.e. to call vs. to respond).
- Discuss different purposes for which music is used (weddings, dancing, listening, movie background music, etc.)

note: see page 45 for solution to Nia Drum Circle Maze

Vocabulary:
1. Nia
2. purpose

Explore Purpose
- In a role-playing exercise have students choose a school job they might like (principal, librarian, cafeteria worker, nurse, etc.) and recite its purpose as they see it. Example: "As a counselor, my purpose is to..."
- Share your thoughts with the students about your purpose as their teacher.

Arts and Crafts Idea *(Graphic Banners)*
- Create *graphic banners* of future goals using felt and material scraps. Consider having students use their short and long-term goals statements from page 11. Hang the banners somewhere where they can be used for inspiration as well as for decoration.

Extending Purpose...

...to the classroom: Start the school day by allowing students to state their purpose for the day. Have them look for opportunities to help others with their stated purposes throughout the course of the day. Review at the close of the day.

...to the family: Have students plan for a real or imagined family outing. What purposeful steps need to be taken for the outing to happen? Have them find out the goals of their family members. What can they do to help family members achieve their goals?

...to the community: How can reaching an individual goal help the community?

© Charphelia Publications

Kuumba

(CD TRACK 6)

                Kuumba, Kuumba
                Creativity, Kuumba

Verse Line 1} She likes to finger-paint
                And hang her pictures on the wall

Verse Line 2} He likes to rap and rhyme
                And make you laugh until you fall

Verse Line 3} She likes to dance around
                Do crazy motions with her feet

Verse Line 4} He likes to strike the drum
                And make it thump a funky beat

                Kuumba, Creativity
                Kuumba, Creativity

                What do you like to do
                To set your mind and body free
                Just to express yourself
                And feel your creativity?

                It doesn't matter if
                It's big in popularity
                It only matters that
                You feel your creativity

                Do you like to paint?
                Do you like to dance?
                Do you like to play a new beat?
                Don't you hesitate
                To jump up at the chance
                To show your creativity

                La la la la la la la la la la la, La-a-la

                What you create
                Not only brings you joy or gives you pride

                The picture's larger than
                The way it makes you feel inside

                'Cause those cool creations
                That maybe pop up in your mind
                Have the potential to
                Improve the rest of humankind

© Charphelia Publications

The sixth principle of Kwanzaa is *Kuumba* (koo-OOM-bah)

Kuumba = Creativity

PLAY CD TRACK 6
Kuumba

The sixth day of Kwanzaa
(December 31)

I use my imagination to make my world a better and more beautiful place.

The song states, "It only matters that you feel your creativity..."

Name one or more ways creativity brings joy to you and to others.
(Write your answer below)

© Charphelia Publications

Song Puzzler

Fill in the missing words from the song *Kuumba*.

1. She likes to finger-paint and hang her _____ on the wall.

2. He likes to _____ and rhyme, and make you laugh until you fall.

3. What do you like to do to set your mind and body _____.

4. Just to express yourself and _____ your creativity.

5. What you create not only brings you _____ and gives you pride.

6. The picture's larger than the way it makes you feel _____.

© Charphelia Publications

Kuumba Phrase

Table

A	B	C	D	E	F	G	H	I	J
22	5	26	13	1	20	16	8	10	15

K	L	M	N	O	P	Q	R	S	T
18	7	12	23	25	3	24	11	2	19

U	V	W	X	Y	Z	.	?
21	6	14	17	4	9	28	27

To create the *Kuumba Phrase,* use the table to write the correct letters and punctuation mark below.

$\overline{14}$ $\overline{8}$ $\overline{22}$ $\overline{19}$ $\overline{26}$ $\overline{22}$ $\overline{23}$

$\overline{10}$

$\overline{26}$ $\overline{11}$ $\overline{1}$ $\overline{22}$ $\overline{19}$ $\overline{1}$ $\overline{19}$ $\overline{25}$ $\overline{13}$ $\overline{22}$ $\overline{4}$ $\overline{27}$

Using the same alphabet table shown above, create your own phrase puzzle on a separate sheet of paper.

© Charphelia Publications

36

In honor of the principle of Kuumba, let your creativity flow.
Here is the beginning of a doodle. How will you complete it?
What can you do with it after you are finished?

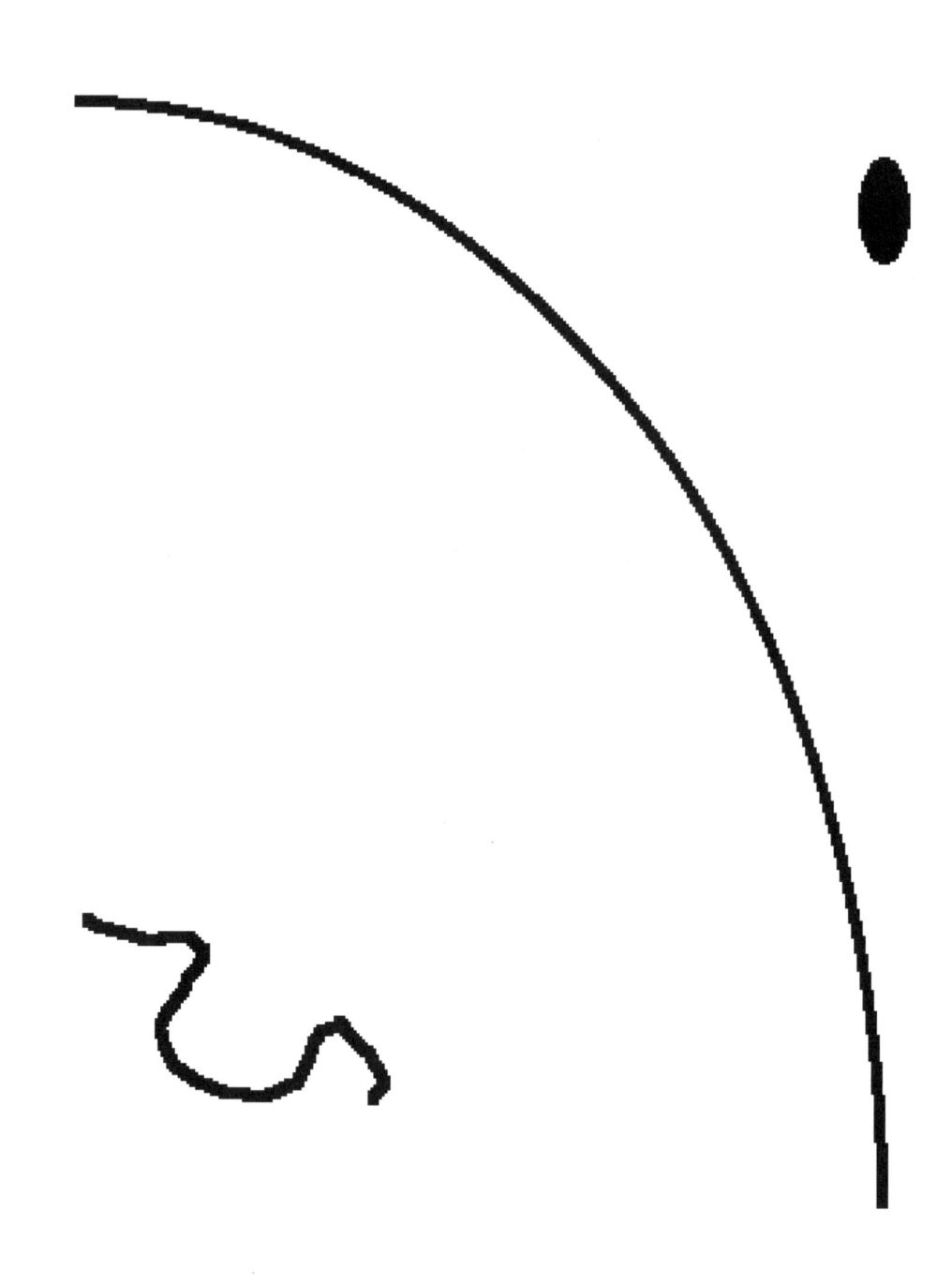

© Charphelia Publications

Teacher Directions

Extending into Music
Music and lyrics are often combined to produce creative works (songs, musicals, operas, etc.).
- **Listen to CD Track 6.**
- Have students compose a lyric line (in the style of verse lines 1 through 4) that says something about their creative likes. Example: "I like to play the flute..."
- Have students sing their lines.

Results: *Open-Ended Doodle*
- Have students name the completed doodles.
- Share doodles in a gallery-walk where students are free to display and view works.

Vocabulary:
1. creativity
2. express
3. hesitate
4. Kuumba
5. potential

Arts and Crafts Idea *(Creative Paperweights)*
- Have students shape clay in their own creative fashions.
- Allow for freedom to reshape.
- Encourage embellishment of clay piece with objects, words, paint and/or pictures. The goal is creative expression.

Extending Creativity...
...to the classroom: Allow opportunities for creative expression in many ways. Encourage children to approach other subjects in a creative way (write a song about multiplication, paint a picture about metamorphosis, etc.).
...to the family: Have students share examples of how family members have expressed creativity (hobbies, recipes, talents, etc.).
...to the community: Can students find examples of creative individuals in the community? Provide a list of artists and have them use the school library to do research. Encourage them to identify and interview other expressers of creativity (a city planner, a tile layer, a chef, etc.).

© Charphelia Publications

Imani

(CD TRACK 7)

Sometimes you'll wonder
If you will be all you can be
And doubts can cloud your hopes and your dreams

It's natural to ponder
How you will turn out in the end
Have faith
You're a child of God
And you are strong
And you were put here to win

Have faith in yourself
In family and God
Believe in your dreams
Imani

Live life by that faith
And not by your fear
And strong you will be
Imani

Sometimes you'll stumble
You'll make a mistake or you'll fall
And fear can shake your heart and your soul

Let this keep you humble
But don't let it keep you knocked down
Stand tall
There's a plan for you
You can't give up
If you want to see it come true

Have faith in yourself
In family and God
Hold fast to your dreams
Imani

Live life led by faith
And not by your fear
And you will be free
Imani

© Charphelia Publications

The seventh principle of Kwanzaa is *Imani* (ee-MON-ee)

Imani = Faith

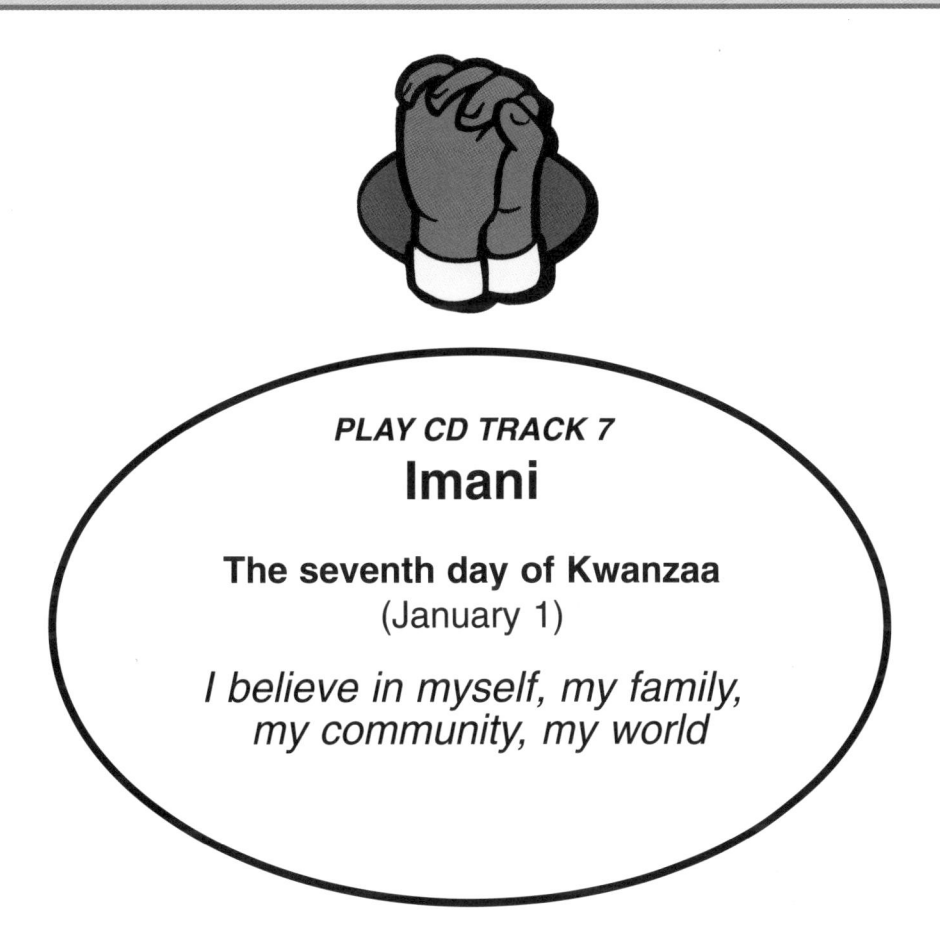

PLAY CD TRACK 7
Imani

The seventh day of Kwanzaa
(January 1)

I believe in myself, my family, my community, my world

The song says, "Have faith in yourself..."

How can having faith help you achieve your dreams?
(Write your answer below)

© Charphelia Publications

Song Puzzler

Circle the correct words from the song *Imani*.

1. It's *(fun, natural)* to ponder.

2. And you were put here to *(lose, win)*.

3. Have faith in *(yourself, homework)*.

4. *(Believe, Play)* in your dreams.

5. Sometimes you'll *(vacuum, stumble)*.

6. You can't *(give, grow)* up.

© Charphelia Publications

Share and Discuss

Faith

What does faith mean to you?

Write down three things that you have faith in and tell why:

1.

2.

3.

Share and discuss your answers.

IMANI CRISS-CROSSWORD

Fill in each blank with the correct word from the puzzle to complete the sentence.

Example: Don't let your <u>doubts</u> stop you from trying.

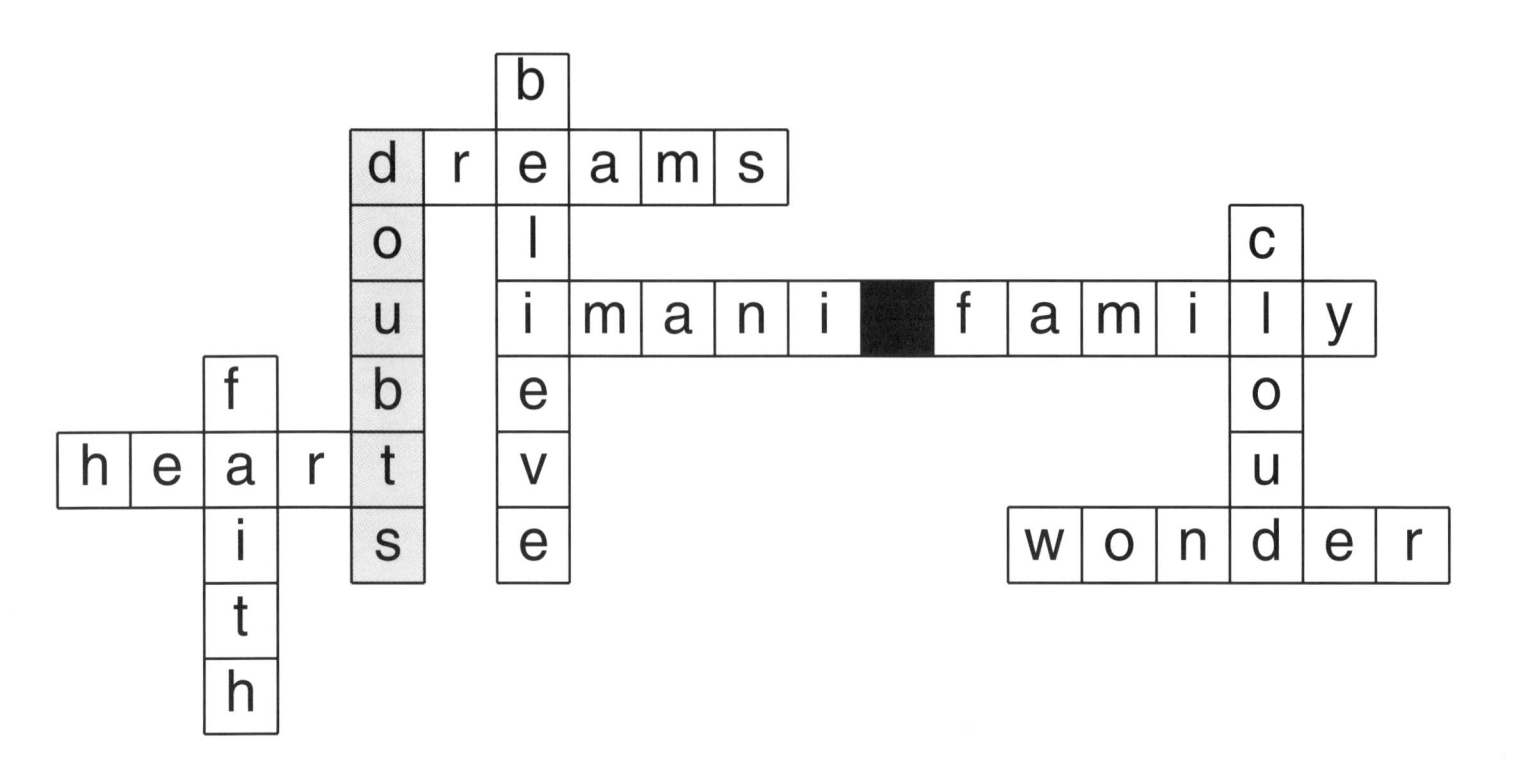

1. Do you _____ in magic?

2. At bedtime, my mother tells me to have sweet _____.

3. The seventh principle of Kwanzaa is _____.

4. I _____ how long the rain will last.

5. When I run, my _____ beats faster.

6. Our _____ took a trip last summer.

7. I looked into the sky and saw a beautiful white _____.

8. Imani means _____.

© Charphelia Publications

Teacher Directions

Extending into Music
Music and lyrics are often used to convey messages about faith (spirituals, hymns, etc.).
- **Listen to CD Track 7.**
- Discuss the song lyrics, line-by-line, with students.
- What messages do the lyrics convey about faith?

Explore Faith
- Have students make statements about how they make decisions. How do they know when something is right?
- Have students reflect on tactics they use to maintain belief in their ability to win.

Vocabulary:
1. believe
2. doubts
3. faith
4. humble
5. Imani
6. ponder
7. stumble

Arts and Crafts Idea *(Imani Faith Boxes)*
- Have students paint shoe boxes with acrylic paint.
- Allow them to decorate with glitter, beads and feathers.
- Ask children to think of things they can place in the box to represent their beliefs and sources of encouragement (a picture of a loved one, a special rock, a word, etc.).

Extending Faith...

...to the classroom: Demonstrate how children can use positive "self-talk" (affirmations) when faced with a difficult task. Provide examples of success stories of people who overcame challenges through faith. Encourage students to do further research.

...to the family: Have individual students interview family members for similar stories that might be shared in class.

...to the community: Have students identify a cause they believe in. Why do they support it? What contribution do they feel they can make?

© Charphelia Publications

Kwanzaa Dance
(CD TRACK 8)

We'll have a happy Kwanzaa
A joyful time
A heartfelt celebration

The blessings of this Kwanzaa
Are yours and mine
There's an open invitation

To be close
To the ones we love
To remind ourselves
What we're made of

Come along
Come one and all
Be a special part
Of the festival

Umoja!
Kujichagulia!
Ujima!
Ujamaa!
Nia!
Kuumba!
Imani!
Kwanzaa! (first time)
It's Kwanzaa time! (second time)

© Charphelia Publications

Nia Drum Circle Maze

(solution)

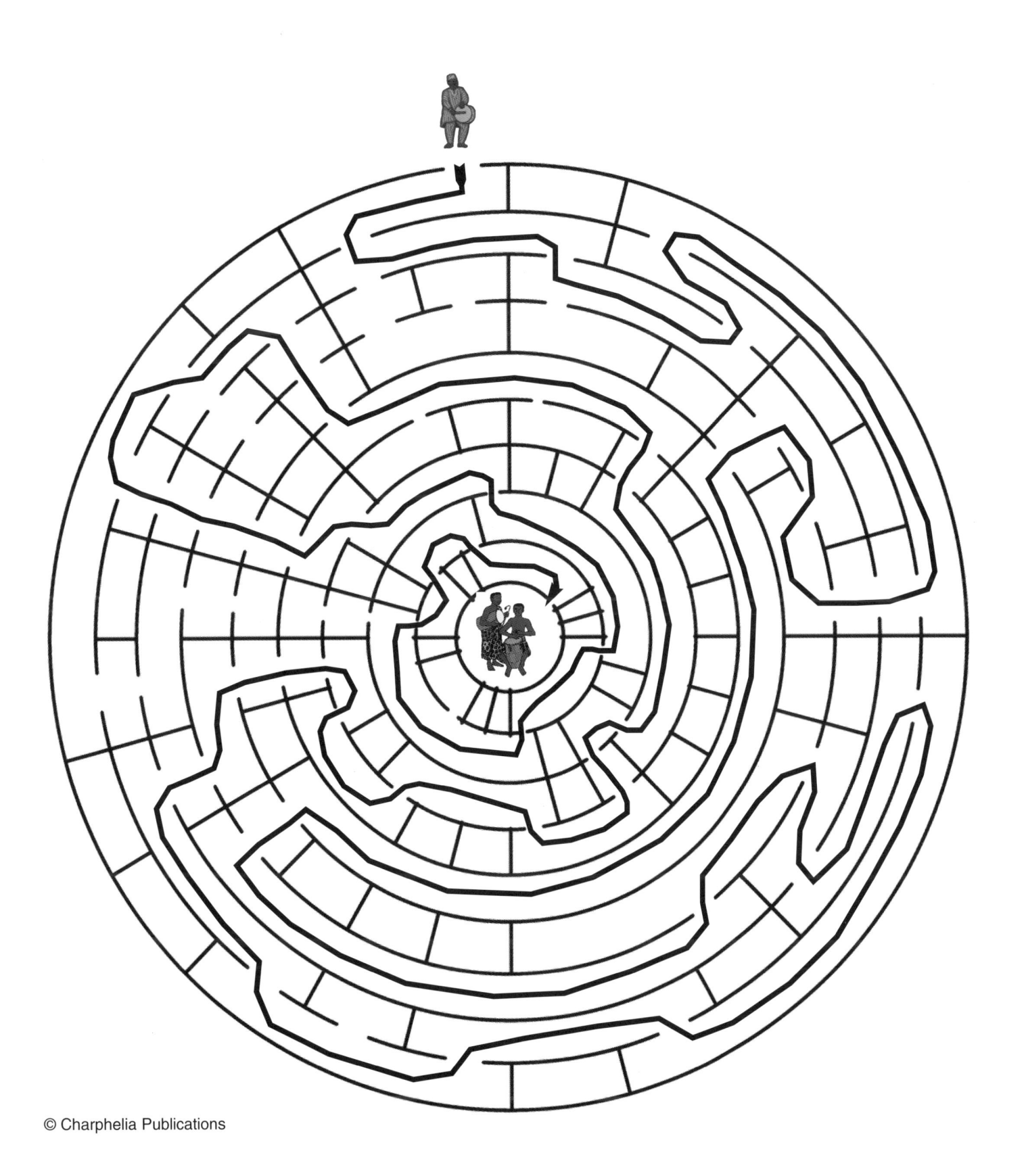

© Charphelia Publications

Quiz #1

Questions

1. What is Kwanzaa?

2. When is Kwanzaa celebrated?

Vocabulary - List and define the principles of Kwanzaa in order.

1. Example: Umoja means unity

2.

3.

4.

5.

6.

7.

Fill in the missing word to the songs.

1. Example: (Kwanzaa Dance) "There's an open <u>invitation.</u>

2. (Ujima) "We help each other by working _____."

3. (Kuumba) "It doesn't matter if it's _____ in popularity."

4. (Imani) "There's a _____ for you."

True or False

___ 1. Martin Luther King created Kwanzaa.

___ 2. Kwanzaa is a celebration of first fruits.

___ 3. Dr. Karenga studied the harvest festivals of Africa.

___ 4. Kwanzaa was created in 1866.

© Charphelia Publications

Quiz #2

Questions

1. In what ways does your family cooperate?

2. Why do you think that Dr. Karenga felt a need to create an African American holiday?

3. Which principle of Kwanzaa means the most to you and why?

4. How can you apply the seven principles to your daily life for the rest of the year, after the Kwanzaa celebration has ended?

5. What are the goals you see for your community? What would you like to change? How would you change it?

© Charphelia Publications

Kwanzaa Journal

1. Umoja
(*Unity*)

_____
_____
_____
_____
_____
_____
_____
_____

2. Kujichagulia
(*Self-Determination*)

_____
_____
_____
_____
_____
_____
_____
_____

Kwanzaa Journal

3. Ujima
(*Collective Work and Responsibility*)

_____
_____
_____
_____
_____
_____
_____
_____

4. Ujamaa
(*Cooperative Economics*)

_____
_____
_____
_____
_____
_____
_____
_____

Kwanzaa Journal

5. Nia
(*Purpose*)

6. Kuumba
(*Creativity*)

Kwanzaa Journal

7. Imani
(Faith)

Kwanzaa
(Kwanzaa)

NOTES